First-Grade Math Minutes

One Hundred Minutes to Better Basic Skills

Written by

Kim Cernek

Editor
Marsha Elyn Wright

Illustrator
Corbin Hillam

Cover Illustrator
Rick Grayson

Designers
Moonhee Pak and Mary L. Gagné

Cover Designer
Barbara Peterson

Art Director
Tom Cochrane

Project Director
Carolea Williams

Reprinted 2009
© 2002 Creative Teaching Press, Inc., Huntington Beach, CA 92649

Table of Contents

Introduction 3

How to Use This Book 4

Scope and Sequence 7

Math Minutes 8

Answer Key 108

Introduction

The focus of *First-Grade Math Minutes* is math fluency—teaching students to solve problems effortlessly and rapidly. The problems in this book provide students with practice in key areas of first-grade math instruction, including

- counting
- basic addition and subtraction facts
- money
- graphing
- patterning
- place value
- measurement
- fractions
- time
- calendar
- flat and solid shapes

First-Grade Math Minutes features 100 "Minutes." Each Minute consists of ten classroom-tested problems for students to try to complete in one minute. Most of the problems in each Minute are grouped in pairs or clusters to give students adequate practice with each new skill. Because each Minute includes questions of varying degrees of difficulty, the amount of time students need to complete each Minute will vary at first.

Use this comprehensive resource to improve your students' overall math fluency, which will promote greater self-confidence in their math skills as well as provide the everyday practice necessary to succeed in a testing situation. With practice, students will improve their own fluency in a manageable, nonthreatening format. The quick format combined with instant feedback makes this a challenging and motivational assignment students will look forward to each day. Students become active learners as they discover mathematical relationships and apply acquired understanding to the solution of grade-appropriate problems in each Minute.

How to Use This Book

First-Grade Math Minutes is designed to be implemented in numerical order. Students who need the most support will find the order of skills as introduced most helpful in building and retaining confidence and success. For example, the first time basic subtraction facts are introduced, number lines for counting back are provided. Eventually, students are asked to compute subtraction facts without the support of a number line.

The Minutes can be used in a variety of ways.

- Use a Minute once for teaching or reviewing a concept and a second time for students to complete on their own within a given a time limit.
- Call out time by the minute as students work on the problems, and have students write on their paper the time called when they finish the Minute.
- Work on a Minute together as a whole-class activity.
- Have students work on a Minute in sections, and establish a time limit based on the type of problems.
- Use a Minute a day for warm-up activities, bell-work, review, assessment, or homework.

Keep in mind that students will get the most benefit from their daily Minute if they receive immediate feedback. If you assign the Minute as homework, correct it in class at the beginning of the day. If you use a Minute as a timed activity, place the paper facedown on the students' desks, or display it as a transparency. Use a clock or kitchen timer to measure one minute. Encourage students to concentrate on completing each problem successfully and not to dwell on problems they cannot complete. At the end of the minute, have students stop working. Then, read the answers from the answer key (pages 108–112), or display them on a transparency. Have students correct their own work and record their score on the Minute Journal reproducible (page 6). Then, have the class go over each problem together to discuss the solution. Spend more time on problems that were clearly challenging for most of the class. Tell students that difficult problems will appear on future Minutes and that they will have other opportunities for success.

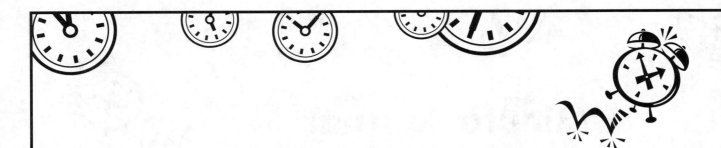

Initially, most first graders will need longer than a minute to complete a page. To assist those students who have difficulties in math, provide multiple choice or true/false answers for long calculation problems. Also, teach students strategies for improving their scores, especially if you time their work on each Minute. Tell students to

- move quickly down the page and answer any problems they know
- work on the more difficult problems as time permits
- come back to problems they are unsure of after they have completed all other problems
- make educated guesses when they encounter problems they are not familiar with
- rewrite word problems as number problems

The Minutes are designed to improve math fluency and should not be included as part of a student's overall math grade. However, the Minutes provide an excellent opportunity for you to see which skills the class as a whole needs to practice or review. This knowledge will help you plan the content of future math lessons. A class that consistently has difficulty with counting money, for example, may make excellent use of your lesson in that area, especially if they know they will have other opportunities to achieve success in this area on future Minutes. Have students file their Math Journal and Minutes for that week in a location accessible to you both. Class discussions of the problems will help you identify which math skills to review. However, you may find it useful to review the Minutes on a weekly basis before sending them home with students at the end of the week.

While you will not include student Minute scores in your formal grading, you may wish to recognize improvements by awarding additional privileges or offering a reward if the entire class scores above a certain level for a week or more. Showing students that you recognize their efforts provides additional motivation to succeed!

Minute Journal

Name _____

Minute	Date	Score	Minute	Date	Score	Minute	Date	Score	Minute	Date	Score
1			26			51			76		
2			27			52			77		
3			28			53			78		
4			29			54			79		
5			30			55			80		
6			31			56			81		
7			32			57			82		
8			33			58			83		
9			34			59			84		
10			35			60			85		
11			36			61			86		
12			37			62			87		
13			38			63			88		
14			39			64			89		
15			40			65			90		
16			41			66			91		
17			42			67			92		
18			43			68			93		
19			44			69			94		
20			45			70			95		
21			46			71			96		
22			47			72			97		
23			48			73			98		
24			49			74			99		
25			50			75			100		

First-Grade Math Minutes © 2002 Creative Teaching Press

Scope and Sequence

SKILL	MINUTE IN WHICH SKILL FIRST APPEARS
Counting	1
Patterns	1
Ordinals (through fifth)	1
Ordering Numbers 0–50	3
Number Words (through twenty)	4
Greater Than or Less Than	4
Using Pictures to Add Sums	5
Money (pennies, nickels, dimes, quarters)	6
Number Sense (before, between, after)	7
Addition (sums to 20)	8
Place Value (tens and ones)	9
Adding Doubles (sums to 20)	9
Counting by 2s, 5s, 10s	9
Plane Figures	11
Addition Sentences	13
Solid Figures	13
Open and Closed Shapes	15
Counting Mixed Collections of Pennies, Nickels, Dimes, Quarters	16
Ordering Numbers 50–100	18
Two-Digit Numbers	19
Single-Digit Subtraction (differences to 9)	21
Calendar	21
Counting Back	21
Counting On (1, 2, 3)	21
Telling Time	21
Even and Odd Numbers	26
Identifying Location (inside, outside, on)	28
Identifying Equal Parts of a Whole	29
Graphs (picture, vertical, horizontal)	30
Measurement (length and height)	31
Nonstandard Measurement	33
Fact Families	36
Digital Time	36
Addition (three addends)	37
Subtracting Tens and Ones without Regrouping	42
Fractions (halves, thirds, fourths)	42
Exploring the Concept of a Dozen	46
Real-Life Addition Problems	46
Measuring Weight (pounds)	52
Measuring Length (inches)	55
Measuring Capacity (cups, pints, quarts)	56
Measuring Length (centimeters)	58
Measuring Capacity (liters)	61
Adding Tens and Ones without Regrouping	61
Ordering Numbers Least to Greatest	61
Lines of Symmetry	78
Measuring Weight (kilograms)	79
Finding Area of a Given Shape	82
Using a Map to Solve Problems	88
Concept of Division	96
Using Data to Make Predictions	98
Concept of Multiplication	99
Making Graphs	99
Comparing Temperatures (hot and cold)	99

Minute 1

Name _____

Write how many shapes there are.

1. ☆☆☆☆ _____

2. ○○○○○○ _____

Draw what comes next in the pattern.

3. ○△○△○ _____

4. □♡□♡ _____

5. Draw 3 cookies.

6. Draw 5 apples.

7. Draw a box around the first shape. ○ □ △ ◇ ▭

8. Draw a circle around the third shape.

Draw an X over the one that does not belong.

9.

A   B   C   D

10.

A   B   C   D

First-Grade Math Minutes © 2002 Creative Teaching Press

Minute 2

Name _____

Write how many shapes.

1. ⚪⚪⚪⚪⚪
   ⚪⚪⚪⚪⚪   _____

2.    _____

Draw what comes next in the pattern.

3. □△□△   _____ _____

4. ○▽○▽   _____ _____

5. Draw 4 legs on the mouse.   **6.** Draw 6 legs on the ant.

7. Letter H is _____.

T	H	I	N	K
1st	2nd	3rd	4th	5th

8. Letter N is _____.

Draw an X over the picture that does not belong.

9.
   A   B   C   D

10.
   A   B   C   D

Minute 3

Name _____

Write the number.

1. IIII = _____

2. one = _____

Draw what comes next in the pattern.

3.  _____ _____

4. _____ _____

5. Draw 8 legs on the spider.　　**6.** Draw 12 legs on the caterpillar.

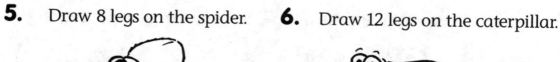

7. The letter _____ is <u>first</u>.　　L　E　A　R　N

8. The letter _____ is <u>third</u>.

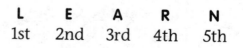

Write the missing number.

9. 1, 2, _____, 4, 5, 6

10. 5, 6, 7, _____, 9

First-Grade Math Minutes © 2002 Creative Teaching Press

Minute 4

Name _____

Write the number.

1. six = _____

2. nine = _____

Draw what comes next in the pattern.

3. ○ ◁ □ ○ ◁ _____ _____ _____

4. □ △ ○ □ _____ _____

5. Draw 10 dots on the ladybug.

6. Draw 4 buttons on the coat.

Circle the picture that shows more:

7.

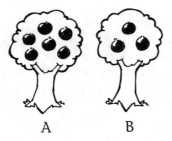

A   B

8.

A   B

Write the missing numbers.

9. 8, 9, _____, 11, _____

10. 7, _____, 5, _____, 3

Minute 5

Name _____

Write the number.

1. ten = _____

2. fifteen = _____

Draw what comes next in the pattern.

3. ↑ ↓ ↑ ↓   _____ _____

4. ▢ ⊠ ▢ ⊠   _____ _____

Add.

5. 4 + 3 = _____   **6.** 3 + 2 = _____

Circle the group that shows <u>more</u>:

7.

A   B

8.

A   B

Write the missing numbers.

9. _____, 16, 17, 18, _____

10. _____, 15, 14, _____, 12

First-Grade Math Minutes © 2002 Creative Teaching Press

Minute 6

Name _____

Write the number.

1. ||||| ||||| = _____

2.   thirteen = _____

Circle the number that is <u>greater</u>:

3.   4   2

4.   3   5

Count backwards. Write the missing numbers.

5.   10   9   _____   _____   _____   _____   4

6.   19   18   _____   _____   _____   _____   13

Add.

7.   3 + 1 = _____   **8.**   4 + 2 = _____

Underline the name of the coin.

9.   penny   nickel   dime   quarter

10.   penny   nickel   dime   quarter

First-Grade Math Minutes © 2002 Creative Teaching Press

Minute 7

Name _____

Write the number.

1. |||| |||| |||| | = _____

2. eighteen = _____

Circle the number that is <u>greater</u>:

3. 15   12

4. 31   21

Write the numbers that come <u>before</u> and <u>after</u>.

5. _____ 25 _____

6. _____ 32 _____

Add.

7. 5 + 3 = _____

8. $\begin{array}{r} 7 \\ +1 \\ \hline \end{array}$

Underline the name of the coin.

9. penny   nickel   dime   quarter

10. penny   nickel   dime   quarter

First-Grade Math Minutes © 2002 Creative Teaching Press

Minute 8

Name _____

Write the number.

1. ||||| ||||| ||||| ||||| = _____

2. fifteen = _____

Circle the number that is less:

3. 44   41

4. 50   47

Look at the first number. Circle the greater number.

5. 35   53   29

6. 27   23   72

Use the number line to add.

7. 8 + 2 = _____

8.   7
   +1

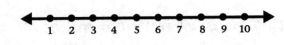

Count. Write the amount.

9. _____ ¢

10. _____ ¢

First-Grade Math Minutes © 2002 Creative Teaching Press

Minute 9

Name _____

Write the number.

1. 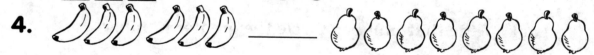 = _____   = _____

2. = _____   = _____

Use > (greater than) or < (less than).

3. ☐ ☐ ☐ _____ ○ ○

4. 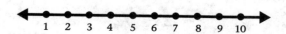 _____

Use the number line to add.

5. 4 + 4 = _____   1 2 3 4 5 6 7 8 9 10

6.   5
   + 5

Count by twos. Write the numbers.

7. _____

8. _____ _____ _____ _____

Count. Write the amount.

9. 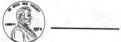 _____ ¢   10. _____ ¢

First-Grade Math Minutes © 2002 Creative Teaching Press

Minute 10

Name _____

Write the number.

1. [base-ten rods] = _____   [unit cubes] = _____

2. [base-ten rods] = _____   [unit cube] = _____

Use > (greater than) or < (less than).

3. |||| |||| _____   [ten rod] [3 cubes]

4. 43 _____ 34

Use the number line to add.

5. 7 + 0 = _____

1 2 3 4 5 6 7 8 9 10

6.   5
      + 4
      ___

Count by fives. Write the numbers.

7. _____ _____ [hands]

8. _____ _____ _____ _____ [hands]

Count. Write the amount.

9. [coins] _____ ¢

10. [coins] _____ ¢

First-Grade Math Minutes © 2002 Creative Teaching Press

Minute 11

Name _____

Look at the first shape. Circle the matching shape.

1. ○   □ △ ○

2. ▽   □ ▽ ○

Circle the coin you need to buy each:

3.
A   B   C

4.
A   B   C

Count by twos. Write the missing numbers.

5. 2   4   _____   _____   _____

6. 12   _____   _____   18   _____

Add.

7. 7 + 3 = _____

8. $\begin{array}{r} 2 \\ + 2 \\ \hline \end{array}$

Write how many of each shape are in the picture.

9. □   _____

10. △   _____

First-Grade Math Minutes © 2002 Creative Teaching Press

Minute 12

Name _____

Write how many of each shape are in the picture.

1. ○ _____

2. ▭ _____

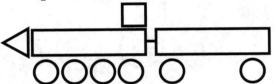

Circle the coin you need to buy the candy:

3.    A B C

4.    A B C

Add.

5. 6 + 3 = _____

6.   4
      + 4
      ‾‾‾

Write the numbers that come before and after.

7. _____ 30 _____

8. _____ 42 _____

Count by tens. Write the numbers.

9. _____ _____ _____

10. _____ _____ _____ _____

Minute 13

Name _____

Look at the first shape. Draw an X over the shape that does not belong.

1.
A B C

2.
A B C

Circle the coins you need to buy the food:

3.

4.

Write the number sentence.

5. _____ + _____ = _____

6.   _____ + _____ = _____

Count by fives. Write the missing numbers.

7. 5 _____ 15 _____

8. 20 _____ _____ 35

Write how many of each shape are in the picture.

9. _____

10. _____

First-Grade Math Minutes © 2002 Creative Teaching Press

Minute 14

Name _____

Look at the first shape. Draw an X over the shape that does not belong.

1.

                A   B   C

2.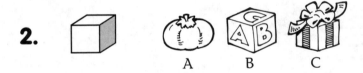

                A   B   C

Use > (greater than) or < (less than).

3.  _____   **4.** _____

Write the number sentence.

5. _____ + _____ = _____

6. _____ + _____ = _____

Count by twos. Write the missing numbers.

7.   2   4   _____   8   _____

8.   _____   6   8   _____   12

Write how many of each shape are in the picture.

9. ▢ _____   **10.** ○ _____

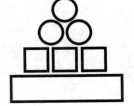

Minute 15

Name _____

1. Circle the shape with three sides: ☐ △ ○

2. Circle the shape with no sides: ☐ △ ○

Use > (greater than) or < (less than).

3. _____

4. _____

Finish the number sentence.

5. ? + = _____ + 2 = 5

6. + ? = 3 + _____ = 8

Copy the closed shape.

7. **8.**

Count by tens. Write the missing numbers.

9. 10 20 _____ _____ 50

10. _____ 60 _____ 80 90

First-Grade Math Minutes © 2002 Creative Teaching Press

Minute 16

Name _____

1. Tally the ◯s. _____

◯ ◯ ◯ ◯ ◯

2. Tally the △s. _____

△ △ △ △ △ △ △ △

Finish the number sentence.

3. 卌 + ? = 卌 |||| 5 + _____ = 9

4. ? + ||| = 卌 |||| _____ + 3 = 9

Count. Write the amount.

5. _____ ¢

6. _____ ¢

Draw an X over the shape that does not belong.

7. A   B   C   D

8. A   B   C   D

Count by twos or fives. Write the missing numbers.

9. _____ 30 35 _____ 45

10. 14 16 _____ 20 _____

First-Grade Math Minutes © 2002 Creative Teaching Press

Minute 17

Name _____

1. Tally the $\square$s. _____

$\square$ $\square$ $\square$ $\square$ $\square$ $\square$ $\square$ $\square$ $\square$ $\square$

2. Tally the ▭s. _____

▭ ▭ ▭ ▭

Write the number sentence.

3. _____ + _____ = _____

4. _____ + _____ = _____

Count. Write the amount.

5. _____ ¢

6. _____ ¢

7. Circle the open shape:

    A   B   C   D

8. Draw an open shape.

Count by twos or tens. Write the missing numbers.

9. _____ 20 _____ 24 26

10. 40 _____ 60 _____ 80 90

First-Grade Math Minutes © 2002 Creative Teaching Press

Minute 18

Name _____

1. Tally the ⊕s. _____

⊕ ⊕ ⊕ ⊕ ⊕ ⊕ ⊕

2. Tally the ⊕s. _____

⊕ ⊕ ⊕ ⊕ ⊕ ⊕ ⊕ ⊕ ⊕ ⊕ ⊕ ⊕ ⊕

Write the number sentence.

3. _____ + _____ = _____

4. _____ + _____ = _____

Count. Write the amount.

5. _____ ¢

6. _____ ¢

7. Circle the closed shape. 3 ○ ∿ ◎
A   B   C   D

8. Draw a closed shape.

Write the numbers that come <u>before</u> and <u>after</u>.

9. _____ 37 _____

10. _____ 50 _____

First-Grade Math Minutes © 2002 Creative Teaching Press

Minute 19

Name _____

1. Tally the ☐s. _____

2. Tally the ☐s. _____

Add.

3. 3 + 3 = _____   **4.**   2
                                      + 4
                                      ____

Count. Write the amount.

5.  _____ ¢

6. _____ ¢

7. Write two-digit numbers using 1 and 5. _____ _____

8. Which number is greater: 17 or 71? _____

Write the numbers that come before and after.

9. _____ 18 _____

10. _____ 63 _____

First-Grade Math Minutes © 2002 Creative Teaching Press

Minute 20

Name _____

Write > (greater than) or < (less than).

1. _____

2. _____

Add.

3. 4 + 3 = _____

4.   5
     + 2

Count. Write the amount.

5. _____ ¢

6. _____ ¢

Copy the closed shape.

7.

8.

9. Write two-digit numbers using 3 and 2. _____ _____

10. Which number is greater: 43 or 34? _____

Minute 21

Name _____

Look at the calendars. Write the missing dates.

1.

Sun.	Mon.	Tues.	Wed.	Thurs.	Fri.	Sat.
	1	_____	3	4	_____	6

2.

Sun.	Mon.	Tues.	Wed.	Thurs.	Fri.	Sat.
16	17	_____	19	_____	21	22

3. 6 + 2 = _____

4.
```
  12
+  2
```

5. Circle the closed shape:

6. Draw a closed shape.

7. Circle the minute hand on the clock:

8. What number does the hour hand point to? _____

Use the number line to count back.

9. 3 − 1 = _____

10. 5 − 1 = _____

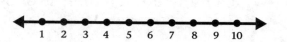

28

Minute 22

Name _____

Look at the calendars. Write the missing dates.

1.

Sun.	Mon.	Tues.	Wed.	Thurs.	Fri.	Sat.
_____	2	3	_____	5	_____	7

2.

Sun.	Mon.	Tues.	Wed.	Thurs.	Fri.	Sat.
23	24	_____	_____	27	_____	29

3.   3 + 4 = _____

4.   11
         + 2
         ‾‾‾

Write the time.

5.   ____ : ____

6.   ____ : ____

Use the number line to count back.

7.   3 – 2 = _____

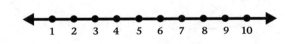

8.   5 – 2 = _____

Circle the coins you need to buy the toy:

9.

         A   B   C   D   E   F

10.

         A   B   C   D   E   F

Minute 23

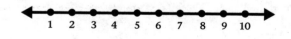

Name _____

Sunday   Monday   Tuesday   Wednesday   Thursday   Friday   Saturday

1. Draw a circle around the day that comes <u>before</u> Tuesday.

2. Draw a box around the day that comes <u>after</u> Thursday.

3. $9 + 3 =$ _____

4. $\begin{array}{r} 10 \\ +\ 2 \\ \hline \end{array}$

Draw the hour hand to show the time.

5. 6:00   (clock)   **6.** 1:00   (clock)

Use the number line to count back.

7. $5 - 3 =$ _____

8. $4 - 3 =$ _____

9. Write two-digit numbers using 7 and 8. _____ _____

10. Which number is greater: 89 or 98? _____

First-Grade Math Minutes © 2002 Creative Teaching Press

Minute 24

Name _____

March   April   May   June   July

1. Draw a circle around the month that comes <u>before</u> June.

2. Draw a box around the month that comes <u>after</u> June.

3. 4 + 5 = _____

4. 14
       + 2
      ‾‾‾‾

Write the time.

5.

    _____ : _____

6.

    _____ : _____

Use the number line to count back.

7. 5 − 1 = _____

8. 2 − 2 = _____

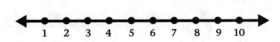

Count by tens. Write the missing numbers.

9. 60   70   _____   _____   100

10. 12   22   _____   42   _____

Minute 25

Name _____

1. Draw a circle around the day of the birthday party.

APRIL						
SUN.	MON.	TUES.	WED.	THURS.	FRI.	SAT.
		1	2	3	4 🧁	5
6	7	8	9	10	11	12
13	14	15	16	17	18	19

2. What day of the week is April 7? _____

Draw what comes next in the pattern.

3. △ ▯ ○ △ ▯ ○ _____ _____

4. ▢ ▢ △ ▢ ▢ _____ _____

5. 9 + 3 = _____

6. 10
   + 4
   ‾‾‾

Draw the minute hand to show the time.

7.
11:00

8.
9:30

Use the number line to count back.

9. 3 − 2 = _____

10. 4 − 2 = _____

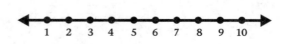

Minute 26

Name _____

January   February   March   April

1. Draw a circle around the month that comes <u>before</u> February.

2. Draw a box around the month that comes <u>after</u> March.

3. Draw an X over the <u>even</u> numbers.   2   3   4   5   6

4. Draw a circle around the <u>odd</u> numbers.   9   10   11   12   13

5. $3 + 2 =$ _____   **6.** $\begin{array}{r} 12 \\ +\ 3 \\ \hline \end{array}$

7. Draw the <u>hour</u> hand to show the time.

| 5:00 |

8. Draw the <u>minute</u> hand to show the time.

| 2:30 |

Use the number line to count back.

9. $5 - 5 =$ _____

10. $2 - 2 =$ _____

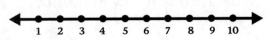

Minute 27

Name _____

SUN.	MON.	TUES.	WED.	THURS.	FRI.	SAT.
☀	🌤	🌧	🌧	🌤	🌧	☀

1. Tally the number of rainy days.

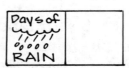

2. Tally the number of sunny days.

3. 6 + 6 = _____

4.
$$
\begin{array}{r}
8 \\
+\,8 \\
\hline
\end{array}
$$

Use the number line to count back.

5. 10 – 5 = _____

6. 10 – 2 = _____

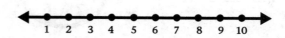

Write the time.

7. ____ : ____

8. ____ : ____

9. Write the missing <u>even</u> numbers.

22, _____, 26, _____, 30

10. Write the missing <u>odd</u> numbers.

41, _____, 45, _____, 49

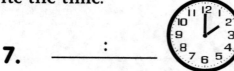
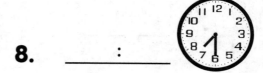

Minute 28

Name _____

SUN.	MON.	TUES.	WED.	THURS.	FRI.	SAT.
6	First Day of CAMP 7	8	9	10	CAMP ENDS 11	12

1. Draw a circle around the day of the week that camp begins.

2. Write the total number of days at camp. _____

3. Draw a circle around the ball that is <u>inside</u> the triangle.

4. Draw an **X** over the ball that is <u>outside</u> the triangle.

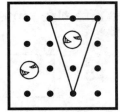

5. $9 + 9 =$ _____

6. $\begin{array}{r} 7 \\ + 7 \\ \hline \end{array}$

Circle the time that the clock shows:

7. 4:30   5:30

8. 1:30   2:30

Use the number line to count back.

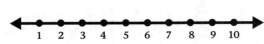

9. $7 - 1 =$ _____

10. $\begin{array}{r} 5 \\ - 1 \\ \hline \end{array}$

Minute 29

Name _____

Sunday	Monday	Tuesday	Wednesday	Thursday	Friday	Saturday
1st	2nd	3rd	4th	5th	6th	7th

1. The 5th day of the week is _____ .

2. The 1st day of the week is _____ .

3. $6 + 6 =$ _____   4. $\begin{array}{r} 4 \\ + 4 \\ \hline \end{array}$

Write the time.

5. 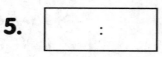   6.

7. $\begin{array}{r} 5 \\ - 0 \\ \hline \end{array}$ 8. $2 - 0 =$ _____

How many equal parts are in each shape?

9. 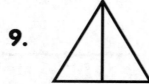 _____ parts

10. 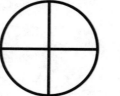 _____ parts

First-Grade Math Minutes © 2002 Creative Teaching Press

Minute 30

Name _____

Children Who Like Peanut Butter

LIKE							

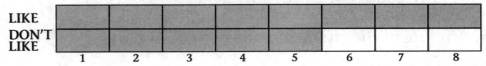

LIKE
DON'T LIKE

   1   2   3   4   5   6   7   8

1. How many children like peanut butter? _____ children

2. How many children do not like peanut butter? _____ children

How many equal parts are in each shape?

3. _____ parts   **4.** _____ parts

Write the time.

5. [:   ]   **6.** [:   ]

Look at the first shape. Circle the matching shape.

7.

                             A   B   C

8.   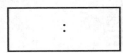

                             A   B   C

9.
$$\begin{array}{r} 5 \\ -\,2 \\ \hline \end{array}$$

10.
$$\begin{array}{r} 4 \\ -\,2 \\ \hline \end{array}$$

Name _____

1. How many equal parts are in the shape?_____

2. Draw a line in the circle to make two equal parts.

Children Who Like Pickles

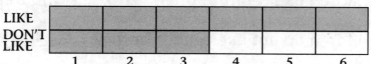

LIKE
DON'T LIKE

1   2   3   4   5   6

3. How many children like pickles? _____ children

4. How many children do not like pickles? _____ children

Circle the longer crayon:

5.  A

BLUE B

6.

A   B

7.
$$\begin{array}{r} 7 \\ -\ 2 \\ \hline \end{array}$$

8. 8 − 2 = _____

Circle the greater amount of money:

9.

A

B

10.

A

B

First-Grade Math Minutes © 2002 Creative Teaching Press

Minute 32

Name _____

1. 11
       + 1

2. 12 + 1 = _____

Favorite Activity at Recess

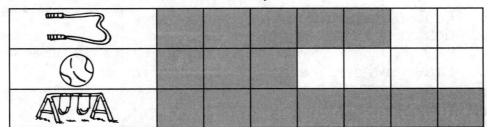

3. Draw a circle around the <u>most</u> favorite activity.   rope   ball   swing

4. Draw an X over the <u>least</u> favorite activity.   rope   ball   swing

Draw a line in each shape to make two equal parts.

5. [rectangle]

6. [circle]

Circle the shortest pencil:

7.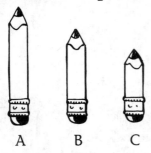

A   B   C

8.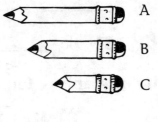

A

B

C

Draw an X over the shape that does not belong.

9.

10.

Minute 33

Name _____

1.   16
       + 0

2.   7
        + 0

Favorite Dessert

3.   Draw a circle around the most favorite dessert.

4.   Draw on **X** over the least favorite dessert.

Write the length.   = 1 unit

5.    = _____ units

6.    = _____ units

Write the missing <u>even</u> numbers.

7.   _____, 22, _____, 26, 28

8.   34, 36, _____, _____, 42

Write how many tens and ones there are.

9.

tens	ones

10.

tens	ones

First-Grade Math Minutes © 2002 Creative Teaching Press

Minute 34

Name _____

1. Draw an X over the marble that is <u>outside</u> the rectangle.

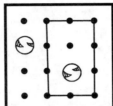

2. Draw a circle around the marble that is <u>inside</u> the rectangle.

Favorite Zoo Animal

lion								
seal								
snake								

3. What is the most favorite animal? _____

4. What is the least favorite animal? _____

Write the length.   ▭ = **1 unit**

5. = _____ units

6. = _____ units

Write how many tens and ones there are.

7.

tens	ones

8.

tens	ones

Use the number line to count back.

9. $\begin{array}{r} 6 \\ -\ 3 \\ \hline \end{array}$

10. $\begin{array}{r} 4 \\ -\ 3 \\ \hline \end{array}$

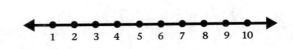

Minute 35

Name _____

1. $7 + 7 =$ _____ **2.** $\begin{array}{r} 9 \\ +\,9 \\ \hline \end{array}$

3. How many children like a car?
_____ children

4. How many more children like a train than a car?
_____ more children

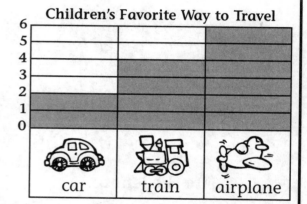

Children's Favorite Way to Travel

Write the length. |———| = 1 inch

5.  = _____ inches

6.  = _____ inches

Draw a line in each shape to make two equal parts.

7.  **8.** ⟨shape⟩

9. $\begin{array}{r} 8 \\ -\,5 \\ \hline \end{array}$ **10.** $\begin{array}{r} 10 \\ -\,5 \\ \hline \end{array}$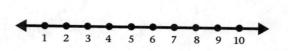

First-Grade Math Minutes © 2002 Creative Teaching Press

Minute 36

Name _____

1. ⬜⬜⬜⬜⬜⬜⬜⬜ + ⬜⬜⬜ = _____

2. ⬜⬜⬜⬜⬜⬜⬜⬜ + ⬜⬜⬜⬜⬜ = _____

Circle the coins you need to buy the toy:

3. You buy 27¢

    A   B   C   D   E   F

4. You buy 18¢   A   B   C   D   E   F

5.  + = _____ ¢

6. + = _____ ¢

Write the time.

7. _____ : _____

8. _____ : _____

Finish the fact family.

9. $4 + 5 = 9$ $9 - 4 = $ _____

10. $5 + 4 = 9$ $9 - 5 = $ _____

Minute 37

Name _____

1. ⬜⬜⬜⬜⬜⬜⬜⬜⬜ + ⬜⬜⬜⬜⬜⬜ = _____   **3.**   4
                                                                                1
2. ⬜⬜⬜⬜⬜⬜⬜⬜⬜ + ⬜⬜⬜⬜⬜⬜⬜ = _____   + 3
                                                                            ─────

Circle which costs more:

4. cow   dolphin

5. elephant   bird

Write the height. ├──┤ = 1 unit

6. _____ units

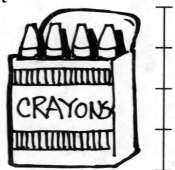

7. _____ units

Finish the fact family.

8. 3 + 5 = 8   8 − 3 = _____   **9.** 5 + 3 = 8   8 − 5 = _____

10. Write the time. _____ : _____

First-Grade Math Minutes © 2002 Creative Teaching Press

Minute 38

Name _____

1.
```
   1
   5
 + 3
```

2.
```
  10
+ 10
```

Circle the coins you need to buy the toy:

3.
A   B   C   D   E

 22¢

4.
A   B   C   D   E

 13¢

5. How many books did each child read?

Tyler _____   Katie _____

Ben _____

6. Who read the most books?

_____

7. Who read the least books?

_____

Books Read			
8			
7	▓		
6	▓	▓	
5	▓	▓	
4	▓	▓	▓
3	▓	▓	▓
2	▓	▓	▓
1	▓	▓	▓
	Tyler	Katie	Ben

8. Write the time. _____ : _____

9. 1 hour <u>before</u> was _____ : _____ .

10. 1 hour <u>after</u> will be _____ : _____ .

Minute 39

Name _____

Finish the fact family.

1. 4 + 3 = 7   3 + 4 = _____

2. 7 – 4 = 3   7 – 3 = _____

3. How many points does Team A have? _____

4. How many points does Team B have? _____

	Team A	Team B

Game 1	||||| ||
Game 2	||||
Game 3	||||| |||||

5. How many points were scored in Game 1? _____ points

6. Which game had the most points?
   _____

7. Circle the order of the trees: shortest to tallest   tallest to shortest

8. Draw the trees in order from tallest to shortest.

9.
```
   9
 – 9
```

10.
```
  10
 – 2
```

First-Grade Math Minutes © 2002 Creative Teaching Press

Minute 40

Name _____

1.
```
   3
   2
 + 4
```

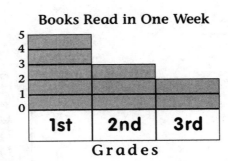

Books Read in One Week

Grades

2. How many books did the second grade read? _____ books

3. How many books did the third grade read? _____ books

4. How many more books did the first grade read than the second grade? _____ more books

5. How many books were read in all? _____ books

Finish the fact family.

6. $5 + 6 = 11$ $6 + 5 =$ _____

7. $11 - 5 = 6$ $11 - 6 =$ _____

8. Write the time. _____:_____

9. 1 hour <u>before</u> was _____:_____ .

10. 1 hour <u>after</u> will be _____:_____ .

First-Grade Math Minutes © 2002 Creative Teaching Press

Minute 41

Name _____

1. $1 + 2 + 1 =$ _____

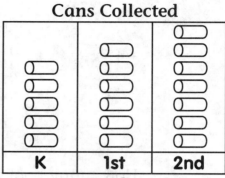

Cans Collected

K	1st	2nd

= 1 can

Grades

2. How many cans did the first grade collect? _____ cans

3. How many cans did the second grade collect? _____ cans

4. How many more cans did the second grade collect than the first grade? _____ more can(s)

5. How many cans were collected in all? _____ cans

Finish the fact family.

6. $8 + 2 = 10$ $2 + 8 =$ _____

7. $10 - 8 = 2$ $10 - 2 =$ _____

8. Write the time. ____ : ____

9. 1 hour <u>before</u> was ____ : ____ .

10. 1 hour <u>after</u> will be ____ : ____ .

First-Grade Math Minutes © 2002 Creative Teaching Press

Minute 42

Name _____

1. $2 + 4 + 2 =$ _____ **2.** $12 + 4 =$ _____

3. $\begin{array}{r} 16 \\ +\ 1 \\ \hline \end{array}$

Circle the shape that shows halves:

4.

     A   B   C

5.

     A   B   C

6. Write the time. _____

7. 1 hour <u>before</u> was _____.

8. 1 hour <u>after</u> will be _____.

9. $\begin{array}{r} 4 \\ -\ 4 \\ \hline \end{array}$

10. $\begin{array}{r} 14 \\ -\ 3 \\ \hline \end{array}$

Minute 43

Name _____

1. 7 + 7 = _____

2.   11
     + 6

3. 5 + 3 + 2 = _____

Circle the shape that shows thirds:

4.   A   B   C

5.   A   B   C

Circle what comes next:

6. Wednesday   Saturday   Tuesday   Thursday

7. Sunday   Wednesday   Monday   Saturday

Draw a line in each shape to make halves.

8.

9.

10.   14
    − 4

First-Grade Math Minutes © 2002 Creative Teaching Press

Minute 44

Name _____

1. $3 + 3 =$ _____   **2.** $\begin{array}{r} 12 \\ +\ 6 \\ \hline \end{array}$

3. $5 + 1 + 4 =$ _____

Circle the shape that shows fourths:

4.
   A   B   C

5.
   A   B   C

6. Circle the correct order:

June, July, September, August   February, March, April, May

Circle what comes before:

7. Friday   Saturday Thursday Sunday

8. Tuesday   Monday Wednesday Friday

Finish the fact family.

9. $8 + 4 = 12$ $4 + 8 =$ _____

10. $12 - 8 = 4$ $12 - 4 =$ _____

First-Grade Math Minutes © 2002 Creative Teaching Press

Minute 45

Name _____

1. $8 + 8 =$ _____

2. $\begin{array}{r} 8 \\ + 11 \\ \hline \end{array}$

3. $1 + 4 + 2 =$ _____

Circle the shape that shows $\frac{1}{3}$ shaded:

4.
    A   B   C

5.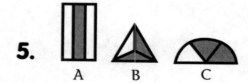
    A   B   C

Color $\frac{1}{3}$ of each shape.

6.    **7.**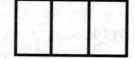

8. Write the time. _____

9. 1 hour <u>before</u> was _____.

10. 1 hour <u>after</u> will be _____.

First-Grade Math Minutes © 2002 Creative Teaching Press

Minute 46

Name _____

1. $3 + 3 =$ _____

2. $\begin{array}{r} 8 \\ + 4 \\ \hline \end{array}$

3. $1 + 5 + 6 =$ _____

4. Circle one <u>dozen</u> stars. 1 dozen = 12

☆☆ ☆☆ ☆☆ ☆☆
☆☆ ☆☆ ☆☆ ☆☆

5. Draw one dozen tallies.   1 dozen = 12

6. You have 3 red crayons and 2 blue crayons. How many crayons do you have in all? _____ crayons

7. $\begin{array}{r} 18 \\ - 7 \\ \hline \end{array}$

8. $\begin{array}{r} 20 \\ - 10 \\ \hline \end{array}$

9. Circle the shape that shows $\frac{1}{2}$ shaded:

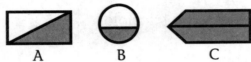

A   B   C

10. Color $\frac{1}{2}$.

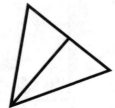

Minute 47

Name _____

1. $2 + 1 + 6 =$ _____

2. $\begin{array}{r} 10 \\ + 4 \\ \hline \end{array}$

3. $3 + 10 =$ _____

4. Circle one <u>dozen</u> eggs. 1 dozen = 12

5. You have 5 white eggs and 3 brown eggs.
How many eggs do you have in all? _____ eggs

Circle the shape that has $\frac{1}{4}$ shaded:

6.
   A   B   C

7.
   A   B   C

8. Color $\frac{1}{4}$ of the shape.

9. Draw an **X** over the ball <u>on</u> the triangle.

10. Draw a circle around the ball
<u>inside</u> the triangle.

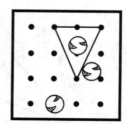

First-Grade Math Minutes © 2002 Creative Teaching Press

Minute 48

Name _____

1. 6
   + 6

2. 12
   + 4

3. 4 + 3 + 2 = _____

4. Circle one dozen doughnuts:

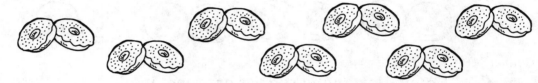

5. You have 2 small doughnuts and 5 large doughnuts.
How many doughnuts do you have in all? _____ doughnuts

Color $\frac{1}{3}$ of each shape.

6. 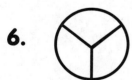 **7.**

Draw the next two beads in the pattern.

8.

9.

10. 16
    − 4

55

Minute 49

Name _____

1. 9
     + 9

2. 18
      + 1

3. 5 + 4 + 1 = _____

4. Count. How many cookies are there in all? _____ cookies

5. You ate 1 cookie. How many cookies are left? _____ cookies

Circle the figures that are the same size and shape:

6. △ △ ☐ ▽ △

7.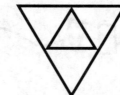

Color $\frac{1}{4}$ of the shape.

8.

9.

10. 18
       − 6

56

Minute 50

Name _____

1. $3 + 2 + 2 =$ _____

2. $\begin{array}{r} 15 \\ + \ 4 \\ \hline \end{array}$

3. How many slices of pizza are there in all? _____ slices

4. You ate 2 slices of pizza. How many slices are left? _____ slices

5. Color $\frac{1}{4}$ of the shape.

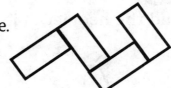

6. Draw lines in the circle to make 4 equal parts.

How many equal parts are shaded?
Circle the matching fraction.

7. $\frac{1}{2}$ $\frac{1}{3}$ $\frac{1}{4}$

8. $\frac{1}{2}$ $\frac{1}{3}$ $\frac{1}{4}$

9. $\begin{array}{r} 15 \\ - \ 5 \\ \hline \end{array}$ **10.** $\begin{array}{r} 19 \\ - \ 7 \\ \hline \end{array}$

Minute 51

Name _____

Finish the fact family.

1. $5 + 7 = 12$ $12 - 7 =$ _____

2. $7 + 5 = 12$ $12 - 5 =$ _____

Draw the clock hands to show the time.

3. 9:00

4. 4:00

Draw a circle around the <u>heavier</u> object.

5.

6.

Draw a circle around the <u>lighter</u> object.

7.

8.

Color $\frac{1}{3}$ of each shape.

9.

10.

Minute 52

Name _____

Finish the fact family.

1. 8 + 3 = 11   11 − 8 = _____   **2.** 3 + 8 = 11   11 − 3 = _____

Draw the clock hands to show the time.

3. 1:00   **4.** 6:00

 = 1 pound

Draw an X over the object that is <u>heavier</u> than 1 pound.

5.    **6.**

Draw a circle around the object that is <u>lighter</u> than 1 pound.

7.    **8.**

9.
```
    3
    1
 + 6
____
```

10. 2 + 5 + 3 = _____

Minute 53

Name _____

Finish the fact family.

1. $8 + 5 = 13$ $13 - 8 =$ _____

2. $5 + 8 = 13$ $13 - 5 =$ _____

Draw a circle around the object that is <u>heavier</u>.

3.   **4.**

Draw a box around the object that is <u>lighter</u>.

5.   **6.**

Draw a circle around the object that holds more.

7.   **8.**

9.   Draw a box around the quarter.

10.   Draw an X over the nickel.

First-Grade Math Minutes © 2002 Creative Teaching Press

Minute 54

Name _____

1. 11
    − 3

2. 12
    − 3

Draw the clock hands to show the time.

3. 1:00

4. 9:30

Draw a circle around the <u>longer</u> object.

5. A CRAYON
    B MARKER

6. A
    B

Draw a box around the object that holds <u>less</u>.

7.

8.

Draw an X over the object that holds <u>more</u>.

9.

10.

Minute 55

Name _____

 = 1 pound

Circle what weighs **less** than 1 pound:

1.   **2.**

Draw the clock hands to show the time.

3. 4:30   **4.** 11:00

Write how many inches long each object is.

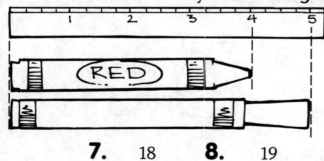

5. crayon = _____ inches

6. marker = _____ inches

7. 18   **8.** 19
    − 8   − 6

Make tally marks to show how many of each object there are.

9. | ball | |
10. | bat | |

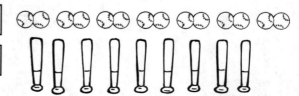

First-Grade Math Minutes © 2002 Creative Teaching Press

Minute 56

Name _____

Count. Write the amount.

1. + = _____ ¢

2. + = _____ ¢

Write how many inches long each object is.

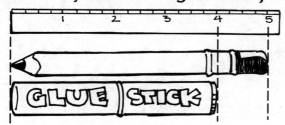

3. pencil = _____ inches

4. glue stick = _____ inches

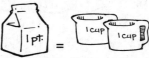

1 pint = 2 cups

Circle how many cups are in each:

5.

6.

Write the number.

7. = _____

8. = _____

9.   16
       – 2

10.   18
        – 4

63

Minute 57

Name _____

Count. Write the amount.

1. 12¢ +  = _____ ¢

2. 11¢ + = _____ ¢

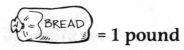

1 pint = 2 cups

Circle how many cups are in each:

3.

4.

Does the object weigh more or less than 1 pound? Underline more or less.

 = 1 pound

5.  more   less   **6.** more   less

7.   3
     4
   + 2

8.   19
     − 5

Draw the clock hands to show the time.

9.
1:30

10.
7:00

First-Grade Math Minutes © 2002 Creative Teaching Press

Minute 58

Name _____

Count. Write the amount.

1. 8¢ +  = _____ ¢   **2.** 10¢ + = _____ ¢

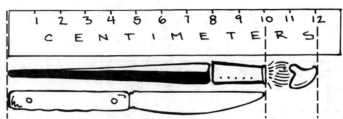

Write how many centimeters long each object is.

3. paintbrush = _____ centimeters

4. knife = _____ centimeters

1 quart = 2 pints

Circle how many pints are in each:

5.

6.

7. 12
    − 1

8. 17
    − 1

Color $\frac{1}{4}$ of each shape.

9.

10.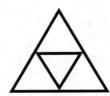

Minute 59

Name _____

Finish the fact family.

1. 4 + 2 = _____   **2.** 2 + _____ = 6

3. 6 − _____ = 4   **4.** 6 − 4 = _____

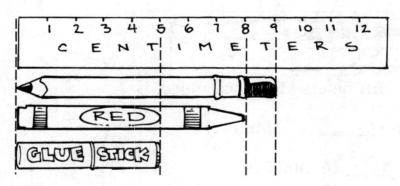

Write how many centimeters long each object is.

5. pencil = _____ centimeters

6. crayon = _____ centimeters

7. glue stick = _____ centimeters

Draw lines in each shape to make 4 equal parts.

8. ☐   **9.** ◯

10. $\begin{array}{r} 28 \\ -\ 5 \\ \hline \end{array}$

First-Grade Math Minutes © 2002 Creative Teaching Press

Minute 60

Name _____

Write the matching fact.

1. $14 - 10 = 4$ $14 - $ _____ $= 10$

2. $12 - 3 = 9$ $12 - $ _____ $= 3$

3. $13 - 6 = 7$ $13 - $ _____ $= 6$

4. $11 - 4 = 7$ $11 - $ _____ $= 4$

 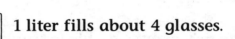 1 liter fills about 4 glasses.

Circle the object that holds <u>more</u> than 1 liter:

5.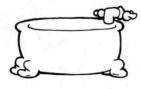

6.

Write how many sides are on each shape.

7. △ _____ sides

8. ☐ _____ sides

9. Draw a shape with 4 sides.

10. Draw a shape with 3 sides.

Minute 61

Name _____

1.   20
       + 10

2.   30
       + 10

3.   30
       − 20

 = 1 liter

Draw an X over the object that holds less than 1 liter.

4.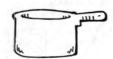

5.

6. Circle the group that has an odd number:

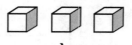
A

B

7. Circle the group that has an even number:

A

B

Write the numbers in order from least to greatest.

8. 13 22 8 1   _____

9. 10 41 35 23 _____

10.   7
           1
         + 8

First-Grade Math Minutes © 2002 Creative Teaching Press

Minute 62

Name _____

1. 35
 + 20

2. 87
 + 10

3. 63
 − 10

Write the numbers in order from least to greatest.

4. 28 18 49 43 _____

5. 50 31 44 40 _____

6. Circle the group that has an <u>odd</u> number:

 ||||| ||||| ||||| ||||| |
 A   B

7. Circle the group that has an <u>even</u> number:

 ||||| ||||| ||||| ||||| ||||| ||||| ||||| ||||| |
 A   B

8. 30
 − 10

9. 20
 − 10

10. 60
 − 10

Minute 63

Name _____

1.　30
　　　+ 20

2.　50
　　　+ 30

3.　70
　　　+ 20

Write the missing numbers.

4.　10,　20,　30,　_____,　_____,　60

5.　50,　60,　_____,　_____,　90

6.　Circle the group that has an <u>odd</u> number:

　　　卌 卌　　　卌 卌 卌
　　　　A　　　　　　B

7.　Circle the group that has an <u>even</u> number:

　　卌 卌 卌 卌　　　卌 卌 卌 卌 卌
　　　　　A　　　　　　　　B

Write the number.

8. = _____

9. = _____

10. = _____

First-Grade Math Minutes © 2002 Creative Teaching Press

Minute 64

Name _____

1.   30
       + 30

2.   20
       + 30

3.   72
       + 10

Write the numbers in order from least to greatest.

4.   35 49 45 30   _____

5.   62 74 50 54   _____

6.   Circle the group that has an <u>odd</u> number:

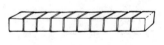

A   B

7.   Circle the group that has an <u>even</u> number:

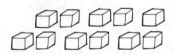

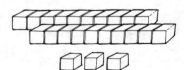

A   B

8.   60
       − 10

9.   40
       − 10

10.   70
        − 10

Minute 65

Name _____

1. 15
     + 30

2. 33
     + 30

3. 42
     + 20

Count. Write the amount.

4. + 3¢ = _____ ¢

5. + 2¢ = _____ ¢

6. Circle the number that is <u>odd</u>:   2   5

7. Circle the number that is <u>even</u>:   2   5

8. 17
     − 10

9. 98
     − 1

10. 44
      − 10

First-Grade Math Minutes © 2002 Creative Teaching Press

Minute 66

Name _____

1.   33
      + 20

2.   42
      + 30

3. Circle what you would use to measure the length of your foot:

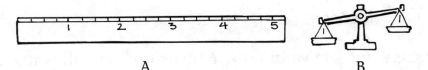

A   B

4. Circle what you would use to measure the weight of an apple:

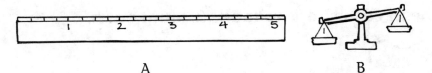

A   B

Count. Write the amount.

5. + 4¢ = _____ ¢

6. + 3¢ = _____ ¢

Circle the shape that shows 2 equal parts:

7.   A   B   **8.**   A   B

9.   42
      − 20

10.   35
       − 20

Minute 67

Name _____

1. 49
      + 20

2. 51
      + 30

3. 38
      + 30

4. Circle what you would use to measure your finger:

inches   feet

5. Circle what you would use to measure how tall you are:

inches   feet

Draw a line in each shape to make 2 equal parts.

6.

7.

8. 55
      − 10

9. 47
      − 20

10. 33
       − 30

First-Grade Math Minutes © 2002 Creative Teaching Press

Minute 68

Name _____

1. Circle the number that is odd: 3   6

2. Circle the number that is even: 3   6

3.   32
       + 22

4.   23
       + 33

5. Circle what you would use to know the time:

A   B

6. Circle what you would use to know the date:

A   B

Underline what is longer.

7.   5 minutes   5 hours

8.   3 days   3 weeks

9.   77
        – 7

10.   55
         – 5

Minute 69

Name _____

1. $\begin{array}{r} 12 \\ + 26 \\ \hline \end{array}$

2. $\begin{array}{r} 28 \\ - 4 \\ \hline \end{array}$

3. $\begin{array}{r} 56 \\ - 22 \\ \hline \end{array}$

4. $3 + 2 + 8 =$ _____

5. Circle what you would use to measure temperature:

      A   B

6. Circle what you would use to measure sugar:

      A   B

Underline what is longer.

7. 2 months   2 weeks

8. 5 months   5 years

Draw two different ways to make 2 equal parts.

9.

10.

First-Grade Math Minutes © 2002 Creative Teaching Press

Minute 70

Name _____

1.　　4
　　　　6
　　　_+ 3_

2.　　44
　　　_− 21_

3.　　43
　　　_+ 34_

Draw two different ways to make 4 equal parts.

4.

5.

6. How many blue marbles were collected?
_____ blue marbles

7. Which color was collected the most? _____

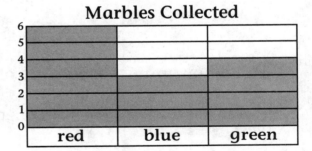

Marbles Collected

8. How many marbles were collected in all? _____ marbles

How many squares cover each shape?

9. 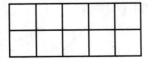　　_____ squares

10.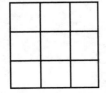

　　　_____ squares

Minute 71

Name _____

1. $1 + 2 = 2 +$ _____

2. _____ $+ 2 = 2 + 3$

Circle the greater amount:

3.

       A   B

4.

       A   B

Write how many corners are on each shape.

5.   _____ corners

6. _____ corners

Draw a line in each shape to make 2 equal parts.

7.

8.

9. $4 + 3 + 3 =$ _____

10. $\begin{array}{r} 38 \\ -\ 22 \\ \hline \end{array}$

First-Grade Math Minutes © 2002 Creative Teaching Press

Minute 72

Name _____

1.   3 + 4 = 4 + _____

2.   _____ + 2 = 2 + 6

Use >, <, or =.

3.   13 _____ 31   **4.**   32 _____ 15

Circle the greater amount:

5.
         A   B

6.
         A   B

7.   Circle the shape with no corners: △   ▭   ○

8.   53
        + 22

9.   98   **10.**   46
        − 50   − 31

Minute 73

Name _____

Finish the fact family.

1. 4 + 7 = _____   **2.** 7 + _____ = 11

3. 11 − _____ = 4   **4.** 11 − 4 = _____

Circle the greater amount:

5. [coins] 22¢
A   B

6. [coins] 5¢ + 5¢ + 10¢
A   B

Use >, <, or =.

7. 13 _____ 10 + 1 + 1

8. 25 _____ 10 + 10 + 5

9. 98
   − 50

10. 45
   − 11

First-Grade Math Minutes © 2002 Creative Teaching Press

Minute 74

Name _____

Write the number.

1. fifteen = _____

2. twenty-one = _____

3. 3 + 3 = 3 + _____

4. 2 + 3 = 3 + _____

Use >, <, or =.

5. $\frac{1}{3}$ _____ $\frac{1}{2}$

6. $\frac{1}{3}$ _____ $\frac{1}{4}$

Write the missing numbers.

7. 15, _____ 25, _____, 35

8. _____, 50, _____, 70, 80

9. 88
   − 40

10. 65
   − 33

Minute 75

Name _____

1. 5 + 2 + 3 = _____   **2.** 3 + 4 + 3 = _____

Use >, <, or =.

3. $\frac{1}{4}$ _____ $\frac{1}{2}$

4. $\frac{1}{3}$ _____ $\frac{1}{2}$

Write the number.

5. 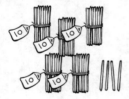 = _____   **6.** 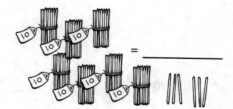 = _____

Draw an X over the heavier object.

7.
   A   B

8.
   A   B

9.   73
       − 52

10.   36
        − 16

First-Grade Math Minutes © 2002 Creative Teaching Press

Minute 76

Name _____

1. 14 – _____ = 7

2. 6 + _____ = 10

3. 3 + 4 + 6 = _____

4. Which grade had the most parties?
_____

5. How many parties did the three grades have altogether?
_____ parties

Popcorn Parties

Grade					
K	✿	✿	✿	✿	✿
1st	✿	✿	✿	✿	
2nd	✿	✿	✿		

Use >, <, or =.

6.

$\frac{1}{2}$ _____ 1

7.

$\frac{1}{2}$ _____ $\frac{1}{4}$

8.
$$\begin{array}{r} 33 \\ -\ 22 \\ \hline \end{array}$$

Circle the shape that does not show 2 equal parts:

9.

A   B   C   D

10.

A   B   C   D

Minute 77

Name _____

Use >, <, or =.

1. 5 + 2 _____ 3   **2.** 3 + 4 _____ 7   **3.** 6 + 7 _____ 15

Money Saved

Joe					
Jill					
Phillip					

4. Who saved the most money? _____

5. How much money did the three children save altogether? $_____

Draw an X over the number that does not belong.

6. 2 4 6 9 12

7. 10 20 25 30 35

8. 36
      − 25

9. 46
      − 11

10. 75
       − 75

First-Grade Math Minutes © 2002 Creative Teaching Press

Minute 78

Name _____

Circle the shape that does not belong:

1.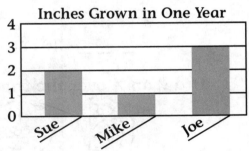

A   B   C

2.

A   B   C

3. Who grew the least amount of inches? _____

4. How many more inches did Joe grow than Mike? _____ inches

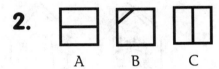

Inches Grown in One Year

Draw an X over the group that does not belong.

5.

A   B   C

6.

A   B   C

Use >, <, or =.

7. $\frac{1}{3}$ _____ $\frac{1}{4}$

8. $\frac{1}{4}$ _____ $\frac{1}{2}$

9.
$$\begin{array}{r} 75 \\ -\ 25 \\ \hline \end{array}$$

10. 5 + 2 + 7 = _____

Minute 79

Name _____

Circle the picture that shows something inside:

1.
A   B

2.
A   B

3. _____ + 10 = 10 + 4

4. 9 + 9 = _____

Draw an X over the fraction that does not belong.

5.

$\frac{1}{2}$ $\frac{1}{2}$ $\frac{1}{3}$

6.

$\frac{1}{4}$ $\frac{1}{3}$ $\frac{1}{4}$

Draw a circle around the object that
weighs less than 1 kilogram.

 = about 1 kilogram

7.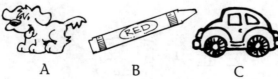
A   B   C

8.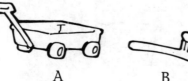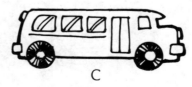
A   B   C

9. $\begin{array}{r} 95 \\ -11 \\ \hline \end{array}$

10. 3 + 6 + 3 = _____

86

First-Grade Math Minutes © 2002 Creative Teaching Press

Minute 80

Name _____

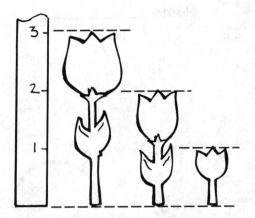

1. How many inches is

the tallest flower? _____ inch(es)

2. How many inches is

the shortest flower? _____ inch(es)

Draw a circle around the object that weighs more than 1 kilogram.

 = about 1 kilogram

3.

   A   B   C

4.

   A   B   C

Draw an X over the shape that does not belong.

5.

  A   B   C   D

6.

 A   B   C   D

Circle the fraction that matches the picture:

7. $\frac{1}{2}$ $\frac{1}{3}$ $\frac{1}{4}$

8. $\frac{1}{2}$ $\frac{1}{3}$ $\frac{1}{4}$

9. _____ + 10 = 10 + 5

10. 5 + 8 + 3 = _____

Minute 81

Name _____

1.   24
        + 10

2.   5 + _____ = 13

Draw the time.

3.

3:00

4.

8:30

Circle the fraction that matches the picture:

5. $\frac{1}{4}$ $\frac{1}{3}$ $\frac{1}{2}$

6. $\frac{1}{4}$ $\frac{1}{3}$ $\frac{1}{2}$

Use >, <, or =.

7. 35 _____ 53

8. 42 _____ 29

9. 2 + 7 + 3 = _____

10.   89
         − 28

First-Grade Math Minutes © 2002 Creative Teaching Press

Minute 82

Name _____

1.   22
       + 33

2.   6 + _____ = 12

3.   1
       4
     + 0

Draw the time.

4. 

4:00

5.

9:30

1st   2nd   3rd   4th   5th

6.   Draw a circle around the third bug.

7.   Draw a box around the fifth bug.

Write how many squares there are in each shape.

8.   The area is _____ squares. 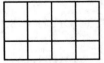

9.   The area is _____ squares. >

10.   Write the area of the shape. 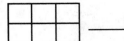 _____ squares

Minute 83

Name _____

1. 41
    + 38

2. 8 + _____ = 16

3. Write the time.

_____ :

4. Draw the time.

10:00

Write the area of each shape.

5. _____ squares

6. _____ squares

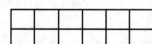

7. Draw a circle inside the square.

8. Draw a triangle outside the square.

9. Draw a star on the square.

10. There are 3 children. Draw a circle around the pie that shows an equal piece for each child.

   A   B   C

Minute 84

Name _____

1. 11
   + 46

2. _____ + 8 = 12

3. Write the time.

_____ : _____

4. Draw the time.

11:30

5. Draw a square outside the triangle.

6. Draw a circle on the triangle.

Use >, <, or =.

7. 49 _____ 26

8. 82 _____ 91

9. 24
   − 12

10. Write the number.

= _____

Name _____

1.
$$\begin{array}{r} 80 \\ + 13 \\ \hline \end{array}$$

2. _____ + 11 = 22

3.
$$\begin{array}{r} 5 \\ 5 \\ + 5 \\ \hline \end{array}$$

4. Draw the time.

3:30

5. Write the time.

_____ : _____

6. Draw a square on the shape.

7. Draw a rectangle outside the shape.

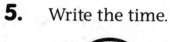

Circle the larger amount:

8.

$\dfrac{1}{2}$ $\dfrac{1}{3}$

9.

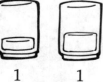

$\dfrac{1}{4}$ $\dfrac{1}{3}$

10.
$$\begin{array}{r} 78 \\ - 33 \\ \hline \end{array}$$

First-Grade Math Minutes © 2002 Creative Teaching Press

Minute 86

Name _____

1. 44
  + 44

2. _____ + 10 = 20

3. 2
  2
  + 2

Circle the shape that does not belong:

4.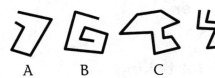

  A   B   C   D

5.

  A   B   C   D

Count the coins. Can you buy the item? Circle *Yes* or *No*.

6. = _____ ¢  Yes   No

7. = _____ ¢   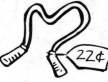  Yes   No

Circle the greater number:

8.   58   85

9.   92   89

10.   Draw 3 equal parts in the shape.

Minute 87

Name _____

1.   14
    + 41

2.   _____ + 10 = 12

3.   2
      0
    + 7

Underline the name that matches the shape.

4.   triangle   cube   cone

5.    square   cube   cone

Circle the group of coins that do not belong:

6.
        A   B   C

7.
        A   B   C

8.   26
    − 14

9.   ____ − 2 = 8

10. Which letter is the fourth letter? _____   E F G H I

Minute 88

Name _____

1. 23
  + 43
  _____

2.   3
    3
  + 3
  _____

3. Circle the pyramid:

4. Circle the sphere:

Blue City

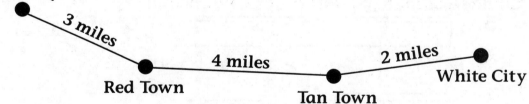

3 miles   4 miles   2 miles

Red Town   **Tan Town**   **White City**

5. How many miles is it from Blue City to Red Town? _____ miles

6. How many miles is it from Red Town to White City? _____ miles

Draw an X over the number that does not belong.

7.   12   10   8   5

8.   19   16   14   12

9.   26
    − 24
  _____

10. Write the number fifty-nine. _____

Minute 89

Name _____

1. _____ + 10 = 10 + 3

2. 8 + 8 = _____

Count the coins. Can you buy the item? Circle *Yes* **or** *No.*

3. 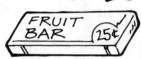 = _____ ¢      Yes   No

4. = _____ ¢   Yes   No

Write how many inches the snail moved.

5. 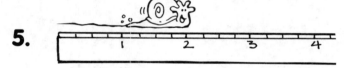 _____ inches

6. 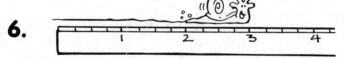 _____ inches

Write what the time was 1 hour <u>before</u>.

7.

1 hour before was _____ : _____ .

9. Write the number sixty-five. _____

8.

1 hour before was _____ : _____ .

10.   60
       − 10

Minute 90

Name _____

1.   33
      + 23
     ———

2.   50 + 20 = _____

Circle the answer:

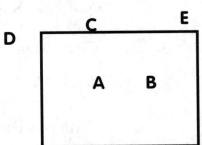

3.   Where is D?   inside   outside   on

4.   Where is C?   inside   outside   on

5.   Where is B?   inside   outside   on

Write what comes next in the pattern.

6.   G H H I G H ____ ____

7.   T U V T U V ____ ____

8.   Write the number forty-three. _____

Write what the time will be 1 hour <u>after</u>.

9.

1 hour after will be _____ : _____ .

10.

1 hour after will be _____ : _____ .

Minute 91

Name _____

1. Draw what comes next in the pattern.

○ ○ ○ □ ○ ○ ○ □ _____ _____ _____

2. Circle the shape that does not belong:

3. Which is the second letter? _____   S T U V W

Write the missing numbers.

4. 21, 22, _____, 24, _____, _____

5. _____, 34, 36, _____, _____, 42

Write the number.

6. seventy-two = _____   **7.** ≣≣≣≣ ≣≣≣≣ = _____

8. 42
     + 13

Use >, <, or =.

9. ≣≣≣≣≣≣ ≣≣≣≣≣≣ _____ ≣≣≣≣ ≣≣≣≣

10. 87 _____ 78

First-Grade Math Minutes © 2002 Creative Teaching Press

Minute 92

Name _____

Use >, <, or =.

1. ‖‖‖‖ ‖‖‖ ‖‖‖ ‖‖‖ ‖‖‖ ‖‖‖ ‖‖‖ ‖‖‖ ‖‖ _____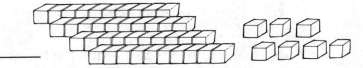

2. 89 _____ 98

3. _____ + 10 = 10 + 9

Write what the time will be 1 hour after.

4. _____ : _____

5. _____ : _____

6. Circle the names of the shapes with 4 sides:

       square   circle   triangle   rectangle

7. Tally the flowers.

Tally Marks

8. 13 + 7 = _____

9.   25
  − 13

10. Circle the greater number: 89   91

First-Grade Math Minutes © 2002 Creative Teaching Press

Minute 93

Name _____

1. Draw an open shape.

2. $4 + 1 = 1 +$ _____

3. Write the dates that are missing.

SUN.	MON.	TUES.	WED.	THURS.	FRI.	SAT.
22	_____	24	25	_____	27	_____

4. Write what the time was 1 hour <u>before</u>.

_____ : _____

5. $3 - 3 =$ _____

6. $12 -$ _____ $= 9$

Candy Bars Sold

	5	10	15	20	25
1st grade	▓	▓	▓	▓	
2nd grade	▓	▓			
3rd grade	▓	▓			

7. How many candy bars did the third grade sell? _____ candy bars

8. Circle the grade that sold the most candy bars:

first grade   second grade   third grade

9. Circle how many candy bars were sold altogether:

20   30   40   50

10.
$$35$$
$$+ 34$$

First-Grade Math Minutes © 2002 Creative Teaching Press

Minute 94

Name _____

1. Draw a closed shape.

2. Circle the day that comes <u>after</u> Thursday:

Monday   Wednesday   Friday

3. Write what the time will be 2 hours <u>after</u>.  ____ : ____

4. Color $\frac{1}{4}$ of the shape.

5. 15 − 15 = _____

6. 98 + 0 = _____

7. Circle $\frac{1}{2}$ of the ladybugs:

8.   92
      − 11

9. Circle the group that has an odd number:

A   B

10. Write the missing numbers.

75, _____, _____, 90, _____, 100

Minute 95

Name _____

1. $3 + 1 + 2 =$ _____

2.
$$\begin{array}{r} 89 \\ -\ 25 \\ \hline \end{array}$$

3. Circle the month that comes <u>before</u> June:

March   May   July

4. $10 +$ _____ $= 7 + 10$

5.
$$\begin{array}{r} 32 \\ +\ 32 \\ \hline \end{array}$$

6. $3 + 11 = 11 +$ _____

7. Write the missing numbers.

_____, 60, _____, _____, 90, 100

8. Circle what you would use to measure the length of your foot:

A   B   C

9. You have 7 cats. You have 4 mats. How many cats do not have a mat? _____ cats

10. Circle the greatest amount:

A   B   C

First-Grade Math Minutes © 2002 Creative Teaching Press

Minute 96

Name _____

1. Write an even number. _____

2. How many days come between Sunday and Saturday? _____ days

   Sunday   Monday   Tuesday   Wednesday   Thursday   Friday   Saturday

3. $76 - 10 =$ _____

4. Draw one dozen hearts. Circle $\frac{1}{2}$.

5. How many hearts are in $\frac{1}{2}$ of a dozen? _____ hearts

6. $10 +$ _____ $= 9 + 10$

7. You have 9 fish. You have 6 fishbowls. How many fish do not have a bowl? _____ fish

8. $30 +$ _____ $= 4 + 30$

9. $\begin{array}{r} 87 \\ -\,14 \\ \hline \end{array}$

10. Write the number ninety-nine. _____

First-Grade Math Minutes © 2002 Creative Teaching Press

Minute 97

Name _____

Write the number.

1. eighty-six = _____   **2.** thirty-one = _____

3. Write the number that comes <u>between</u>.

   78 _____ 80

4. Circle the greater amount: 10¢ + 10¢ + 10¢ + 1¢   or   28¢

5. Circle the pyramid:

6. You have 9 dogs. You have 2 bones. How many dogs do not have a bone? _____ dogs

7. 86 – 10 = _____

8. Write the numbers from least to greatest.

   27 29 30 28   _____ _____ _____ _____

9. 4 + 11 = 11 + _____

10. Circle the shape that has 3 corners:

First-Grade Math Minutes © 2002 Creative Teaching Press

Minute 98

Name _____

1.   43
       − 12

2.   11 + 5 = _____ + 11

Finish the fact family.

3.   3 + 9 = 12   12 − _____ = 3

4.   9 + 3 = 12   12 − 3 = _____

5.   Circle the shape that has no corners: □ ○ △ ▭

6.   Write the time.

       _____ :

7.   2 children want to share 8 apples. Each child gets _____ apples.

8.   40 + 20 = _____

9.   Circle the cube:

10.   What takes more than
        1 minute? Circle *A* or *B*.

A

B

First-Grade Math Minutes © 2002 Creative Teaching Press

Minute 99

Name _____

1. Color in the graph to show how many of each shape there are.

△ ○ □ □ △ ○ ○
□ △ ○ □ ○ △ ○

	Favorite Shape	
7		
6		
5		
4		
3		
2		
1		
0		
△	□	○

2. Circle *hot* or *cold*.

hot   cold

3. Which picture shows what is sure to happen?   Circle *A* or *B*.

A   B

4. How many balls are in each group? _____ balls

5. How many groups are there? _____ groups

6. How many balls are there in all? _____ balls

Write the number.

7. ninety-eight = _____   **8.** fifty-seven = _____

Use >, <, or =.

9. 40 _____ 20 + 20   **10.** 30 _____ 10 + 10

First-Grade Math Minutes © 2002 Creative Teaching Press

Minute 100

Name _____

1. 6 + _____ = 12

2. 30 + 20 = _____

3. How many steps are there from the rock to the pond? _____ steps

4. How many steps are there from the tree to the pond? _____ steps

5. Circle *hot* or *cold*.

hot   cold

6. 11 + _____ = 6 + 11

7. 12 – 2 = _____

Favorite Fruit

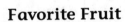

🍎							
🍌							
🍊							

0 1 2 3 4 5 6 7

8. Color in the graph to show how many of each fruit there are.

Which picture shows what is sure to happen? Circle *A* or *B.*

9.

A   B

10.

A   B

Minute Answer Key

Minute 1
1. 4
2. 7
3. △
4. □
5. Student draws 3 cookies.
6. Student draws 5 apples.
7. ○
8. △
9. C
10. B

Minute 2
1. 10
2. 5
3. □, △
4. ○, ▽
5. Student draws 4 legs.
6. Student draws 6 legs.
7. 2nd
8. 4th
9. D
10. B

Minute 3
1. 5
2. 1
3. ○, ▷
4. ▽, ▯
5. Student draws 8 legs.
6. Student draws 12 legs.
7. L
8. A
9. 3
10. 8

Minute 4
1. 6
2. 9
3. □, ○
4. △, ○
5. Student draws 10 dots.
6. Student draws 4 buttons.
7. A
8. B
9. 10, 12
10. 6, 4

Minute 5
1. 10
2. 15
3. ↑, ↓
4. ▢, ⊠
5. 7
6. 5
7. A
8. B
9. 15, 19
10. 16, 13

Minute 6
1. 10
2. 13
3. 4
4. 5
5. 8, 7, 6, 5
6. 17, 16, 15, 14
7. 4
8. 6
9. nickel
10. penny

Minute 7
1. 16
2. 18
3. 15
4. 31
5. 24, 26
6. 31, 33
7. 8
8. 8
9. quarter
10. dime

Minute 8
1. 20
2. 15
3. 41
4. 47
5. 53
6. 72
7. 10
8. 8
9. 7¢
10. 5¢

Minute 9
1. 10, 2
2. 30, 4
3. >
4. <
5. 8
6. 10
7. 2, 4
8. 2, 4, 6, 8
9. 7¢
10. 10¢

Minute 10
1. 40, 5
2. 60, 1
3. <
4. >
5. 7
6. 9
7. 5, 10
8. 5, 10, 15, 20
9. 14¢
10. 17¢

Minute 11
1. ○
2. ▽
3. B
4. C
5. 6, 8, 10
6. 14, 16, 20
7. 10
8. 4
9. 4
10. 4

Minute 12
1. 6
2. 2
3. A
4. C
5. 9
6. 8
7. 29, 31
8. 41, 43
9. 10, 20, 30
10. 10, 20, 30, 40

Minute 13
1. B
2. B
3. 1 dime, 3 pennies
4. 1 nickel, 3 pennies
5. 2 + 4 = 6
6. 5 + 3 = 8
7. 10, 20
8. 25, 30
9. 3
10. 5

Minute 14
1. C
2. A
3. >
4. <
5. 6 + 3 = 9
6. 8 + 2 = 10
7. 6, 10
8. 4, 10
9. 3
10. 3

Minute 15
1. △
2. ○
3. <
4. =
5. 3
6. 5
7. Student copies closed shape.
8. Student copies closed shape.
9. 30, 40
10. 50, 70

Minute 16
1. 𝍸
2. 𝍸 III
3. 4
4. 6
5. 15¢
6. 30¢
7. C
8. D
9. 25, 40
10. 18, 22

Minute 17
1. 𝍸 𝍸 I
2. IIII
3. 6 + 2 = 8
4. 7 + 1 = 8
5. 20¢
6. 22¢
7. B
8. Student draws open shape.
9. 18, 22
10. 50, 70

Minute 18
1. 𝍸 II
2. 𝍸 𝍸 II
3. 3 + 1 = 4
4. 2 + 2 = 4
5. 40¢
6. 14¢
7. B
8. Student draws closed shape.
9. 36, 38
10. 49, 51

Minute 19
1. 𝍸 𝍸 I
2. 𝍸 𝍸 III
3. 6
4. 6
5. 28¢
6. 53¢
7. 15, 51
8. 71
9. 17, 19
10. 62, 64

Minute 20
1. >
2. <
3. 7
4. 7
5. 30¢
6. 31¢
7. Student copies closed shape.
8. Student copies closed shape.
9. 32, 23
10. 43

First-Grade Math Minutes © 2002 Creative Teaching Press

Minute Answer Key

Minute 21
1. 2, 5
2. 18, 20
3. 8
4. 14
5. △
6. Student draws closed shape.
7. Student circles minute hand.
8. 3
9. 2
10. 4

Minute 22
1. 1, 4, 6
2. 25, 26, 28
3. 7
4. 13
5. 5:00
6. 7:00
7. 1
8. 3
9. A, B, E or F
10. A or B, C, E, F

Minute 23
1. Monday
2. Friday
3. 12
4. 12
5. Student draws 6:00.
6. Student draws 1:00.
7. 2
8. 1
9. 78, 87
10. 98

Minute 24
1. May
2. July
3. 9
4. 16
5. 10:30
6. 4:30
7. 4
8. 0
9. 80, 90
10. 32, 52

Minute 25
1. April 4
2. Monday
3. △ , ☐
4. △ , ☐
5. 12
6. 14
7. Student draws 11:00.
8. Student draws 9:30.
9. 1
10. 2

Minute 26
1. January
2. April
3. 2, 4, 6
4. 9, 11, 13
5. 5
6. 15
7. Student draws 5:00.
8. Student draws 2:30.
9. 0
10. 0

Minute 27
1. III
2. II
3. 12
4. 16
5. 5
6. 8
7. 2:00
8. 7:30
9. 24, 28
10. 43, 47

Minute 28
1. Monday
2. 5
3. Student circles ball inside triangle.
4. Student draws X over ball outside triangle.
5. 18
6. 14
7. 4:30
8. 2:30
9. 6
10. 4

Minute 29
1. Thursday
2. Sunday
3. 12
4. 8
5. 8:00
6. 4:30
7. 5
8. 2
9. 2
10. 4

Minute 30
1. 8
2. 5
3. 3
4. 4
5. 11:00
6. 12:30
7. B
8. B
9. 3
10. 2

Minute 31
1. 2
2. Student draws 2 equal parts.
3. 6
4. 3
5. A
6. A
7. 5
8. 6
9. B
10. A

Minute 32
1. 12
2. 13
3. swing
4. ball
5. Student draws 2 equal parts.
6. Student draws 2 equal parts.
7. C
8. C
9. ◁
10. ⊕

Minute 33
1. 16
2. 7
3. cookie
4. cupcake
5. 3
6. 5
7. 20, 24
8. 38, 40
9. 1 ten, 3 ones
10. 3 tens, 4 ones

Minute 34
1. Student draws X over marble outside rectangle.
2. Student circles marble inside rectangle.
3. lion
4. snake
5. 5
6. 4
7. 4 tens, 3 ones
8. 3 tens, 6 ones
9. 3
10. 1

Minute 35
1. 14
2. 18
3. 2
4. 2
5. 2
6. 4
7. Student draws 2 equal parts.
8. Student draws 2 equal parts.
9. 3
10. 5

Minute 36
1. 13
2. 16
3. A, B, C or D, E, F
4. A or B, C, D, E, F
5. 6¢
6. 7¢
7. 9:30
8. 6:30
9. 5
10. 4

Minute 37
1. 17
2. 18
3. 8
4. dolphin
5. elephant
6. 4
7. 2
8. 5
9. 3
10. 2:30

Minute 38
1. 9
2. 20
3. A, B, C, D or E
4. A, C, D, E
5. 7, 6, 4
6. Tyler
7. Ben
8. 3:00
9. 2:00
10. 4:00

Minute 39
1. 7
2. 4
3. 5
4. 3
5. 7
6. 3
7. shortest to tallest
8. Student draws trees in order from tallest to shortest.
9. 0
10. 8

Minute 40
1. 9
2. 3
3. 2
4. 2
5. 10
6. 11
7. 5
8. 7:00
9. 6:00
10. 8:00

Minute Answer Key

Minute 41
1. 4
2. 6
3. 7
4. 1
5. 18
6. 10
7. 8
8. 4:30
9. 3:30
10. 5:30

Minute 42
1. 8
2. 16
3. 17
4. A
5. B
6. 1:30
7. 12:30
8. 2:30
9. 0
10. 11

Minute 43
1. 14
2. 17
3. 10
4. B
5. C
6. Thursday
7. Monday
8. Student draws 2 halves.
9. Student draws 2 halves.
10. 10

Minute 44
1. 6
2. 18
3. 10
4. C
5. A
6. February, March, April, May
7. Thursday
8. Monday
9. 12
10. 8

Minute 45
1. 16
2. 19
3. 7
4. B
5. A
6. Student colors $1/3$.
7. Student colors $1/3$.
8. 5:30
9. 4:30
10. 6:30

Minute 46
1. 6
2. 12
3. 12
4. Student circles 1 dozen stars.
5. ⦀⦀ ⦀⦀ II
6. 5
7. 11
8. 10
9. A
10. Student colors $1/2$.

Minute 47
1. 9
2. 14
3. 13
4. Student circles 1 dozen eggs.
5. 8
6. C
7. B
8. Student colors $1/4$.
9. Student draws X over ball on triangle.
10. Student circles ball in triangle.

Minute 48
1. 12
2. 16
3. 9
4. Student circles 1 dozen doughnuts.
5. 7
6. Student colors $1/3$.
7. Student colors $1/3$.
8. □, ○
9. ○, □
10. 12

Minute 49
1. 18
2. 19
3. 10
4. 8
5. 7
6. △, ▽
7. ○, ○
8. Student colors $1/4$.
9. Student colors $1/4$.
10. 12

Minute 50
1. 7
2. 19
3. 6
4. 4
5. Student colors $1/4$.
6. Student draws 4 equal parts.
7. $1/3$
8. $1/4$
9. 10
10. 12

Minute 51
1. 5
2. 7
3. Student draws 9:00.
4. Student draws 4:00.
5. banana
6. pumpkin
7. balloon
8. empty glass
9. Student colors $1/3$.
10. Student colors $1/3$.

Minute 52
1. 3
2. 8
3. Student draws 1:00.
4. Student draws 6:00.
5. bicycle
6. dog
7. feather
8. toothbrush
9. 10
10. 10

Minute 53
1. 5
2. 8
3. book
4. alligator
5. empty basket
6. empty wagon
7. large pot
8. teapot
9. Student draws box around quarter.
10. Student draws X over nickel.

Minute 54
1. 8
2. 9
3. Student draws 1:00.
4. Student draws 9:30.
5. B
6. A
7. mug
8. small vase
9. large pail
10. large bowl

Minute 55
1. paper
2. ladybug
3. Student draws 4:30.
4. Student draws 11:00.
5. 4
6. 5
7. 10
8. 13
9. ⦀⦀ ⦀⦀ IIII
10. ⦀⦀ IIII

Minute 56
1. 8¢
2. 11¢
3. 5
4. 4
5. 2 cups
6. 4 cups
7. 14
8. 26
9. 14
10. 14

Minute 57
1. 15¢
2. 14¢
3. 4 cups
4. 6 cups
5. more
6. less
7. 9
8. 14
9. Student draws 1:30.
10. Student draws 7:00.

Minute 58
1. 16¢
2. 20¢
3. 12
4. 10
5. 2 pints
6. 4 pints
7. 11
8. 16
9. Student colors $1/4$.
10. Student colors $1/4$.

Minute 59
1. 6
2. 4
3. 2
4. 2
5. 9
6. 8
7. 5
8. Student draws 4 equal parts.
9. Student draws 4 equal parts.
10. 23

Minute 60
1. 4
2. 9
3. 7
4. 7
5. bathtub
6. aquarium
7. 3
8. 4
9. Student draws 4-sided shape.
10. Student draws 3-sided shape.

First-Grade Math Minutes © 2002 Creative Teaching Press

Minute Answer Key

Minute 61
1. 30
2. 40
3. 10
4. cup
5. ladle
6. A
7. B
8. 1, 8, 13, 22
9. 10, 23, 35, 41
10. 16

Minute 62
1. 55
2. 97
3. 53
4. 18, 28, 43, 49
5. 31, 40, 44, 50
6. B
7. A
8. 20
9. 10
10. 50

Minute 63
1. 50
2. 80
3. 90
4. 40, 50
5. 70, 80
6. B
7. A
8. 33
9. 19
10. 28

Minute 64
1. 60
2. 50
3. 82
4. 30, 35, 45, 49
5. 50, 54, 62, 74
6. B
7. A
8. 50
9. 30
10. 60

Minute 65
1. 45
2. 63
3. 62
4. 34¢
5. 39¢
6. 5
7. 2
8. 7
9. 97
10. 34

Minute 66
1. 53
2. 72
3. A
4. B
5. 54¢
6. 46¢
7. A
8. B
9. 22
10. 15

Minute 67
1. 69
2. 81
3. 68
4. inches
5. feet
6. Student draws 2 equal parts.
7. Student draws 2 equal parts.
8. 45
9. 27
10. 3

Minute 68
1. 3
2. 6
3. 54
4. 56
5. B
6. A
7. 5 hours
8. 3 weeks
9. 70
10. 50

Minute 69
1. 38
2. 24
3. 34
4. 13
5. A
6. B
7. 2 months
8. 5 years
9. Student draws 2 ways to make 2 equal parts.
10. Student draws 2 ways to make 2 equal parts.

Minute 70
1. 13
2. 23
3. 77
4. Student draws 2 ways to make 4 equal parts.
5. Student draws 2 ways to make 4 equal parts.
6. 3
7. red
8. 13
9. 10
10. 9

Minute 71
1. 1
2. 3
3. A
4. B
5. 4
6. 3
7. Student draws 2 equal parts.
8. Student draws 2 equal parts.
9. 10
10. 16

Minute 72
1. 3
2. 6
3. <
4. >
5. A
6. A
7. O
8. 75
9. 48
10. 15

Minute 73
1. 11
2. 4
3. 7
4. 7
5. B
6. A
7. >
8. =
9. 48
10. 34

Minute 74
1. 15
2. 21
3. 3
4. 2
5. <
6. >
7. 20, 30
8. 40, 60
9. 48
10. 32

Minute 75
1. 10
2. 10
3. <
4. <
5. 54
6. 76
7. A
8. B
9. 21
10. 20

Minute 76
1. 7
2. 4
3. 13
4. K
5. 12
6. <
7. >
8. 11
9. C
10. D

Minute 77
1. >
2. =
3. <
4. Joe
5. $11
6. 9
7. 10
8. 11
9. 35
10. 0

Minute 78
1. C
2. B
3. Mike
4. 2
5. C
6. B
7. >
8. <
9. 50
10. 14

Minute 79
1. A
2. B
3. 4
4. 18
5. 1/3
6. 1/3
7. B
8. B
9. 84
10. 12

Minute 80
1. 3
2. 1
3. A
4. C
5. D
6. D
7. 1/4
8. 1/3
9. 5
10. 16

First-Grade Math Minutes © 2002 Creative Teaching Press

Minute Answer Key

Minute 81
1. 34
2. 8
3. Student draws 3:00.
4. Student draws 8:30.
5. ¼
6. ⅓
7. <
8. >
9. 12
10. 61

Minute 82
1. 55
2. 6
3. 5
4. Student draws 4:00.
5. Student draws 9:30.
6. spider
7. snail
8. 12
9. 9
10. 6

Minute 83
1. 79
2. 8
3. 5:30
4. Student draws 10:00.
5. 6
6. 12
7. Student draws circle inside.
8. Student draws triangle outside.
9. Student draws star on square.
10. A

Minute 84
1. 57
2. 4
3. 1:30
4. Student draws 11:30.
5. Student draws square outside.
6. Student draws circle on triangle.
7. >
8. <
9. 12
10. 83

Minute 85
1. 93
2. 11
3. 15
4. Student draws 3:30.
5. 7:00
6. Student draws square on shape.
7. Student draws rectangle outside.
8. ½
9. ⅓
10. 45

Minute 86
1. 88
2. 10
3. 6
4. D
5. C
6. 17¢, No
7. 55¢, Yes
8. 85
9. 92
10. Student draws 3 equal parts.

Minute 87
1. 55
2. 2
3. 9
4. cone
5. cube
6. B
7. B
8. 12
9. 10
10. H

Minute 88
1. 66
2. 9
3. △
4. ⊕
5. 3
6. 6
7. 5
8. 19
9. 2
10. 59

Minute 89
1. 3
2. 16
3. 38¢, No
4. 27¢, Yes
5. 2
6. 3
7. 1:30
8. 4:00
9. 65
10. 50

Minute 90
1. 56
2. 70
3. outside
4. on
5. inside
6. H, I
7. T, U
8. 43
9. 10:00
10. 1:30

Minute 91
1. ○, ○, ○
2. ▭
3. T
4. 23, 25, 26
5. 32, 38, 40
6. 72
7. 38
8. 55
9. >
10. >

Minute 92
1. =
2. <
3. 9
4. 4:30
5. 11:00
6. square, rectangle
7. 卌 卌 ||||
8. 20
9. 12
10. 91

Minute 93
1. Student draws open shape.
2. 4
3. 23, 26, 28
4. 1:00
5. 0
6. 3
7. 10
8. first grade
9. 40
10. 69

Minute 94
1. Student draws closed shape.
2. Friday
3. 8:00
4. Student colors ¼.
5. 0
6. 98
7. Student circles 7 bugs.
8. 81
9. B
10. 80, 85, 95

Minute 95
1. 6
2. 64
3. May
4. 7
5. 64
6. 3
7. 50, 70, 80
8. C
9. 3
10. A

Minute 96
1. Student writes an even number.
2. 5
3. 66
4. Student draws 1 dozen hearts and circles 6 of them.
5. 6
6. 9
7. 3
8. 4
9. 73
10. 99

Minute 97
1. 86
2. 31
3. 79
4. 10¢ + 10¢ + 10¢ + 1¢
5. △
6. 7
7. 76
8. 27, 28, 29, 30
9. 4
10. △

Minute 98
1. 31
2. 5
3. 9
4. 9
5. ○
6. 2:00
7. 4
8. 60
9. ▱
10. B

Minute 99
1. Student makes graph.
2. hot
3. A
4. 4
5. 3
6. 12
7. 98
8. 57
9. =
10. >

Minute 100
1. 6
2. 50
3. 6
4. 10
5. cold
6. 6
7. 10
8. Student makes graph.
9. B
10. B

First-Grade Math Minutes © 2002 Creative Teaching Press